TIMES PAST
GREAT CITIES
Sheffield

Top, Left To Right: Smoky Sheffield, 1930s; Shell Workers At Cammell-Laird's, 1916; Town Hall, 1905; Forge Dam, Early 1900s; Bottom: Kemsley House, High Street, 1930s

MELVYN JONES

MYRIAD
LONDON

CITY CENTRE

In 1800 Sheffield was a small town; by the 1920s, when most of the photographs shown here had already been taken, the light steel trades and the heavy steel industry had transformed it into a city of more than half a million people. The city centre reflected this momentous change

ABOVE: **THE ROYAL VISIT OF KING EDWARD VII AND QUEEN ALEXANDRA, 1905.** The visit took place on July 12 to open the new University of Sheffield. The royal carriage stands outside the new town hall that Edward's mother, Queen Victoria, had officially opened on May 21 1897 – which she did by "remote control" without leaving her horse-drawn carriage! She later visited Norfolk Park and Charles Cammell's Cyclops Works to see (still in her carriage) armour plate being rolled "which guards your Empire upon the sea" as the Corporation address put it.

ABOVE: **SHEFFIELD'S NEW TOWN HALL.** Built between 1891-96 and constructed of Derbyshire sandstone, this "picturesque pile" has on its outside walls two friezes depicting Sheffield's industrial history showing among other things grinders, smiths, smelters and miners. The 200ft (61m) tower is surmounted by an 8ft (2.4m) bronze statue of Vulcan, the Roman god of fire and furnaces.

RIGHT: **MOORHEAD, EARLY 1900S.** The photograph shows the view looking back along Pinstone Street towards the town hall on the right. In the left foreground the large building is the department store of T and G Roberts, built in 1882 and destroyed by German bombs on Thursday December 12 1940. Beyond Roberts Brothers' store is the tower of the Salvation Army Citadel and Hostel opened in 1894.

Moor Head, Sheffield.

LEFT AND ABOVE: Exterior and interior views of ST PAUL'S CHURCH, early 1900s. It was designed by members of the Platt family, the Rotherham mason-architects. The building of this church began in 1720 but it did not open (as a chapel of ease for the parish church) until 1740. This was because of an argument between the church authorities and the main donor of money for its construction, John Downes, a goldsmith, about the appointment of the curate. The dome was paid for by public subscription and added in 1769. The church was demolished in 1938 and the site is now occupied by the Peace Gardens.

John Walsh's High Street — Sheffield

ABOVE: The impressive KEMSLEY HOUSE, the Sheffield Telegraph building, completed in 1916, on the corner of York Street and High Street, faced with white faience, and still an important architectural landmark in central Sheffield. The portico, surmounted by a statue of Mercury, led to the newspaper's head office and counting house.

ABOVE: JOHN WALSH'S DEPARTMENT STORE, c 1900. John Walsh opened his first shop in 1875 but had this new store built after the widening of High Street. It opened in 1899. The very top floors were dormitories for shop staff. It was destroyed in the Blitz but was rebuilt after the war.

ABOVE: **SNIG HILL, EARLY 1890S.** The photograph shows the top of Snig Hill on a busy shopping day. The probable meaning of the word "snig" is for a block of wood that was put through cartwheels to act as a brake. The Sheffield Independent printing offices on the left were leased to a surgeon-dentist who was offering a complete new set of teeth for one guinea!

RIGHT: **FITZALAN SQUARE, EARLY 1900S.** The square was then a busy tram terminus with horse cabs for hire. The building in the centre background is the Fitzalan Market Hall. In the right background is the Post Office and the building with the classical columns and tall dome is the office of the Birmingham, Dudley and District Banking Company (later Barclays).

LEFT: **FOSTERS' BUILDINGS, HIGH STREET _c_ 1900.** Linking the markets area in the north with Fargate to the south, High Street was and remains at the core of Sheffield's retail area. A crowded electric open-topped tram (open-topped trams ran until 1911) and a horse bus complete the busy scene.

RIGHT: **LEOPOLD STREET, 1910.** The square building in the background is Firth College, forerunner of the University of Sheffield, and in the foreground is the Grand Hotel (now demolished) which opened in 1910. The hotel contained a lounge where an orchestra entertained, a dining room that accommodated 300 diners, and three self-contained suites.

ABOVE AND LEFT: THE CITY HALL under construction in Barker's Pool, c 1930 and the completed hall opened in 1932. Originally designed as early as 1920, by E.Vincent Harris, construction did not begin until 1929. It is in the Classical Revival style, dominated by the portico with eight Corinthian columns. Originally conceived as a memorial hall to the city's First World War dead it became Sheffield's main concert hall with a memorial hall at the rear. The main hall accommodates 2,800 people.

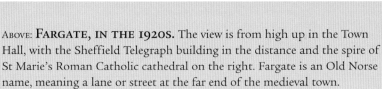

ABOVE: **FARGATE, IN THE 1920S.** The view is from high up in the Town Hall, with the Sheffield Telegraph building in the distance and the spire of St Marie's Roman Catholic cathedral on the right. Fargate is an Old Norse name, meaning a lane or street at the far end of the medieval town.

ABOVE: **THE MARKET AREA, LATE 1950S.** The market area grew up around the Norman castle (largely demolished in the 1640s) at the confluence of the rivers Don and Sheaf. The Norman lord of the manor, Thomas de Furnival, obtained a royal charter in 1296 to hold a market every Tuesday.

HISTORIC LANDMARKS

By the beginning of the 20th century the city centre and its surrounding suburbs were still dotted with landmarks reflecting Sheffield's long manorial, ecclesiastical, industrial and urban history. Although some have been lost in the intervening period through wartime bombing and redevelopment, many interesting examples still survive

RIGHT AND INSET: The medieval **PARISH CHURCH** that became the cathedral in 1914. The most interesting part of the cathedral is the Shrewsbury Chapel that contains the tombs of the 4th and 6th Earls of Shrewsbury. Shown here is the tomb of the 4th Earl (1468-1538). Besides the earl, the tomb has the figures of his two wives, only one of whom is seen here.

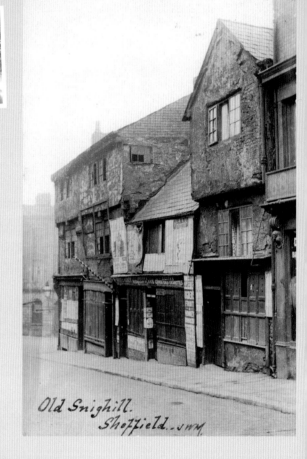

RIGHT: **OLD SNIG HILL** showing surviving medieval timber-framed buildings at the end of the 19th century. These were destroyed as part of a road-widening scheme in the early 1900s.

BELOW: **THE UNIVERSITY OF SHEFFIELD**. The red-brick Tudor-style buildings of Sheffield's new university were opened by King Edward VII on July 12 1905. The commitment to gain full university status for the university college that had started life in 1897 was given fresh impetus when it was suggested that the University College of Leeds should become the University of Yorkshire.

ABOVE: **THE HALL IN THE PONDS**. Now the Old Queen's Head public house, it is one of only a handful of surviving timber-framed buildings in the city. Tree-ring analysis shows that it was constructed of timber felled between 1503-10. It is reputedly named after Mary, Queen of Scots, the legend being that she was brought on visits here by the 6th Earl of Shrewsbury during her captivity in Sheffield between 1570-84.

RIGHT: **LADY'S BRIDGE, EARLY 1900S.** First built in stone in 1486 to replace an earlier timber structure, it marked the northern entrance to the old town over the River Don. The late medieval bridge which is hidden below the modern bridge was built by master mason William Hyll, whose instructions were to "make a sufficient brigge over the watyr of Dune neghe the castell of Sheffield".

BELOW: **THE TURRET HOUSE AT MANOR LODGE.** Mostly in ruins now, only the Turret House, built in the 1570s still survives largely intact. In some accounts it is claimed to be a porter's lodge and in others a secure accommodation for Mary, Queen of Scots.

BELOW: The remains of **BEAUCHIEF ABBEY** in the Sheaf valley in the south of the city which was founded between 1173 and 1176 by Robert FitzRanulf. Beauchief is a Norman-French name meaning "beautiful headland" that refers to the steeply wooded hillside beside the abbey. In the 1660s Edward Pegge of Beauchief Hall converted the abbey church into a private chapel.

LEFT AND BELOW: **SHEPHERD WHEEL** in the Porter valley showing the grinding of cutlery at a water-powered site with an "over-shot" vertical water wheel. This water-powered site was first referred to in the will of Roger Barnsley in 1566. The name Shepherd Wheel is derived from a tenant, Edward Shepherd, who operated the works during the 18th century. It was worked commercially until 1930 and until recently was open to the public by the city's Museums Service.

ABOVE: **BISHOPS' HOUSE** in Meersbrook Park, a splendid timber-framed yeoman's house mainly of 16th-century construction. It was the home of the Blythe family, yeomen farmers and scythe-makers. It became known as Bishops' House because it was believed that two members of the Blythe family who became bishops had been born there.

LIGHT STEEL TRADES

By 1400 Sheffield was famous for its cutlery and over the next five centuries became the world leader in the production of cutlery and a wide range of edge-tools. The claim that "Right Sheffield is best ... excelling the rest" was as true in the early 1900s as it was when it was written in 1590

INTERIOR CRUCIBLE FURNACE " TEEMING."

The Knife Grinders, Sheffield.

ABOVE: **CRUCIBLE STEEL SHOP, EARLY 1900S.** The development of crucible steel-making by Benjamin Huntsman in the 1740s eventually resulted in the world-renown of Sheffield cutlery and an international reputation for Sheffield as a steel-making centre. By 1850 90 per cent of the country's steel was made in Sheffield.

ABOVE AND BELOW: **GRINDERS** who put the cutting edge on cutlery and other edge tools at grindstones powered by water or steam power and who for centuries suffered early deaths through inhaling stone and metal dust, and **BUFFER GIRLS** who gave the products their final high polish.

Metal Buffers, Sheffield.

ABOVE: **THE NORFOLK KNIFE.** This knife was made by Joseph Rodgers & Sons for the Great Exhibition at the Crystal Palace in London in 1851. It stands more than two feet and six inches long and contains more than 70 blades and tools. It is now on permanent loan at the Cutlers' Hall.

ABOVE: **SHEFFIELD CRAFTSMEN AT WORK.** Left to right: Jack Stedman file cutting at Brown Brothers in the 1950s; a scissors maker in the early 1900s; John Thomas Ridge, gimlet maker in Ecclesfield, 1950s. Before the widespread mechanisation of the industry, cutlery manufacture and related trades were mostly in the hands of "little mesters" who ran their own businesses with the help of apprentices and journeymen. In their workshops might be a coal-fuelled smithy where blades were forged or small rooms where the handles were fitted or "hafted"; and where the products were finally assembled after the blades were ground on a grindstone. Even when factories became common, little mesters rented spaces there. One or two little mesters still survive.

ABOVE: **HARRY BREARLEY**, discoverer of stainless steel in 1913. His ground-breaking discovery changed the face of cutlery manufacture after the First World War.

LEFT: **WALKER & HALL'S ELECTRO WORKS, 1920S.** Established in 1845 Walker & Hall was the largest employer in the cutlery trades by the early 1900s employing upwards of 1,000 workers. The firm specialised in electro-plated goods.

HEAVY STEEL INDUSTRY

The heavy steel industry was a relative newcomer to Sheffield. It did not emerge until the 1850s but by the end of the 19th century had overtaken the light steel trades; the result was a vast physical expansion of the urban area together with explosive population growth

ABOVE: **THE LOWER DON VALLEY AT TINSLEY, 1930S.** Growing at a rapid rate to meet the insatiable demand for railway parts, shells and guns, and plates for ships, the heavy steel industry covered the fields in the Lower Don valley in Brightside, Attercliffe and Tinsley with works and housing.

BELOW: **CRUCIBLE MELTING TEAM.** Before 1858 and the adoption of the Bessemer process the only way of making large ingots of steel was to assemble in one works a large number of cementation furnaces and crucible shops.

RIGHT: **CARLISLE STREET, EARLY 1900S.** In the heart of industrial Brightside a vast army of heavy steel workers troop between work and home at the end of the working day. In the 60 years between 1841 and 1901 Brightside's population grew from 10,000 to 75,000.

RIGHT: **BAR ROLLING AND HAMMER FORGING.** Large progressive firms dominated the industry from the beginning. The nature of the industry demanded huge amounts of capital and large-scale mechanised operations. By 1900 there were eight firms employing more than 2,000 men and another six employing between 1,000 and 2,000.

BELOW: **SHEFFIELD ROAD, TINSLEY, 1930S.** The photograph emphasises the close proximity of workplace (WT Flather's steelworks in this case) and home, and the almost complete urbanisation of Sheffield's East End, "that once lovely valley", as one Victorian writer put it.

RIGHT AND BELOW: Three dramatic views of steel making processes at **CAMMELL-LAIRD'S WORKS** during the First World War. On the right a locomotive tyre is being rolled. Below on the left a crucible "teemer", protected by leggings, apron and gloved hand, lifts a crucible with tongs and, using his thigh as a fulcrum, pours the red hot metal into a waiting ingot mould. The skill and strength involved in the intense heat was immense. Below, right, the view is of the production of Bessemer steel introduced to Sheffield by Sir Henry Bessemer in 1858. Using the traditional methods of making steel (converting pig iron into blister steel and then crucible steel) took 14 or 15 days to produce a 40-50 pound ingot of steel, whereas the Bessemer process could produce about six tons of steel in about 30 minutes.

ROLLING A LOCOMOTIVE TYRE.   CAMMELL LAIRD SHEFFIELD

LEFT: **PATTERN SHOP WORKERS, EARLY 1900S** at **VICKERS SONS & MAXIM LTD** and FAR LEFT: **A TEAM WORKING A STEAM HAMMER** in the 1940s at **ENGLISH STEEL'S RIVER DON WORKS.** The manufactures of Vickers included ships, guns, engines, armour plates, castings, railway materials and motor car parts. In 1928 Vickers amalgamated with Cammell-Laird to form the English Steel Corporation and this led to the modernisation of Cammell's Grimesthorpe Works and Vickers' River Don Works. These works made a massive contribution to the country's war effort in both world wars. For example, during the first 18 months of the Second World War the only drop hammer capable of forging Spitfire crankshafts was at the River Don Works. The English Steel Corporation's factories also supplied armour-plating for the country's fighter planes, tanks and battleships, besides gun barrels and bombs.

ABOVE: **HADFIELD'S EAST HECLA WORKS, EARLY 1900S.** This firm, founded in 1875 by Robert Hadfield, was originally based at the Hecla Works in Attercliffe. His son, Sir Robert Hadfield, a brilliant applied scientist, set up the East Hecla Works in 1888 devoted almost entirely to the manufacture of armaments.

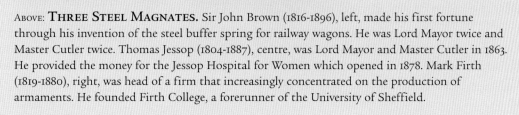

ABOVE: **THREE STEEL MAGNATES.** Sir John Brown (1816-1896), left, made his first fortune through his invention of the steel buffer spring for railway wagons. He was Lord Mayor twice and Master Cutler twice. Thomas Jessop (1804-1887), centre, was Lord Mayor and Master Cutler in 1863. He provided the money for the Jessop Hospital for Women which opened in 1878. Mark Firth (1819-1880), right, was head of a firm that increasingly concentrated on the production of armaments. He founded Firth College, a forerunner of the University of Sheffield.

ABOVE: **MUNITIONS WORKERS** at Firth Brown during the First World War. Production in the heavy steel industry was at a very high level and women for the first time worked in the industry.

PARKS

Sheffield's urban parks – more than a dozen in all – surround the city centre like pearls on a necklace. They vary in age from the early Victorian period to the mid-20th century and often incorporate or lead to informal countryside

BOTANICAL GARDENS.

Frozen Fountain Weston Park Jan 14 1905 – JWM.

ABOVE: **BOTANICAL GARDENS, 1890S.** This was Sheffield's first planned formal green space, opened in 1837, and dominated by its glass pavilions. Originally the central pavilion was a tropical palm house with the two smaller pavilions at either end housing temperate plants.
RIGHT, ABOVE: Ornamental pond, **FIRTH PARK, 1905.** The park, donated by Mark Firth, opened in 1875.
RIGHT, BELOW: Frozen fountain, **WESTON PARK, 1905.** This park was opened in 1875.

BAND STAND

ABOVE: Gardening staff at **WESTON PARK**, early 1900s.

LEFT: **FIRTH PARK, EARLY 1900S.** A large crowd in their Sunday best listen to a concert in the bandstand. It was reported in the 1890s that as many as 1,000 people visited the park every day in spring and summer and on Good Friday 30,000 might be expected.

ABOVE, LEFT: HILLSBOROUGH PARK, 1900. The park, previously the landscaped grounds of a private house, was opened in 1892. The photograph shows the Adam-style Hillsborough House, which became a library, reading room and picture gallery, and the splendid bandstand, now demolished.

ABOVE: ENDCLIFFE PARK, 1905. The park, on land in the Porter valley acquired in 1885, contains a number of "dams", artificial ponds formerly feeding water-powered grinding wheels. Shown here is Holme Wheel Dam, which had become a boating lake by 1900.

LEFT: ECCLESFIELD PARK, AUGUST 1954. Playgrounds have always been important areas in local parks. Most Victorian parks had a "gymnasium" where there would be swings and perhaps a "giant stride", a pole with ropes from which great leaps could be made as it rotated.

RIGHT: WHIT SING, HILLSBOROUGH PARK, EARLY 1900S. It is difficult now to believe the vast numbers involved in Whitsuntide gatherings in the past. The main occasion was the Whit Sing, often in a local park around the bandstand, when hymns that had been practised for many weeks beforehand would be sung with great gusto by adults and children from surrounding churches and chapels. And everyone would be decked out in their Whitsuntide clothes, in Edwardian times, as here, with the women in their splendid hats.

TRANSPORT

The century from 1819 saw a public transport revolution in Sheffield: canals, horse buses, railways, horse trams, electric trams and motor buses all arrived and had a dramatic effect on industrial growth and the physical expansion of the urban area

ABOVE: **THE WICKER RAILWAY ARCHES, 1905.** The arches which carried the Manchester, Sheffield and Lincolnshire Railway into the town in 1845 are bedecked in honour of the visit of King Edward VII to open the new university.

RIGHT: **DARNALL STATION.** By 1900 industrial and residential suburbs were speedily linked by rail to the city centre: Brightside, Attercliffe and Darnall in the east end, Dore and Totley in the south and Wadsley Bridge in the north-west.

RIGHT: **HORSE BUS, 1880S** and BELOW: **HORSE TRAM** *c* 1900. Horse buses came into operation in 1838 from the Moor and Glossop Road to link with the Bridgehouses railway station on the Sheffield to Rotherham Railway that opened in that year. The first horse tram ran from Lady's Bridge to the Golden Ball Hotel in Attercliffe in 1873.

RIGHT: **ILLUMINATED ELECTRIC TRAM, 1911.** The first electric tram service came into use in 1899 but horse trams continued until 1902. This tram is decorated with illuminations in honour of the coronation of King George V.

LEFT: **POND STREET BUS STATION IN THE 1950S.** The first motor buses were out and about on the streets of Sheffield by 1913. A bus loading station at Pond Street came into use in 1936. The photograph must have been taken before 1956 when covered accommodation was built.

ABOVE: **THE LOCK HOUSE, TINSLEY** *c* 1900. The canal terminated at Tinsley in 1751. From there a turnpike road was built into Sheffield six miles away.

LEFT: **SHEFFIELD CANAL BASIN IN THE 1880S.** The canal made a belated entry into the centre of Sheffield in 1819, only 19 years before the arrival of the first railway. The extension of the canal into Sheffield and the opening of the Canal Basin were greeted with acclaim in the town and a fleet of barges with flags and bands made a triumphal entry into the Canal Basin.

LEISURE

As the city's population soared in the second half of the 19th century and new working-class and middle-class communities emerged and stabilised, a wide range of clubs, societies and organised recreational events came into existence

ABOVE. **CHARABANC OUTING,** *c* **1910.** Country and seaside outings became extremely popular with the emergence of the charabanc. This is a trip from the High Greave Hotel, Ecclesfield.

LEFT: **SHARROW CYCLING CLUB,** *c* **1900.** Despite the steep slopes cycling became a very popular pastime in the Sheffield area after the development of the air-filled tyre in 1888 and the mass production of reasonably priced bicycles in the 1890s.

ABOVE: **WOODHOUSE PRIZE BAND, 1888.** Many industrial communities created brass bands in the late 19th century. The bandmaster of the Woodhouse Prize Band is JW Cook, standing on the extreme left of the back row.

ABOVE: **CHAPELTOWN OPERATIC SOCIETY.** Operatic and dramatic societies also became widespread. Here the cast of the society's production of Gilbert & Sullivan's Yeomen of the Guard pose in their colourful costumes in Chapeltown Park.

RIGHT: **CORONATION PARTY, 1953.** The end of wartime hostilities and coronations were celebrated by street parties throughout the city. This is the party in Rutland Street in central Sheffield to celebrate the coronation of Queen Elizabeth II.

BELOW: **SEASIDE STUDIO PORTRAIT, LATE 1890S.** One for the family album! "Dressed to the nines", members of the Greaves family of Cross Hill, Ecclesfield hold their poses in a photographic studio while on holiday in Blackpool.

LEFT: **CHAPELTOWN FEAST AT NIGHT, 1932.** Fairs or "feasts" have always been eagerly awaited events. Besides swings and roundabouts, Chapeltown Feast in the 1930s had the added attraction of a man who put his head into the mouth of a man-eating lion.

BELOW: **SKATING IN WHITELEY WOODS.** The many frozen dams (artificial ponds) in Sheffield's river valleys were an irresistible attraction to ice skaters in hard winters.

19

THIS SPORTING LIFE

Sport, amateur and professional, has long been an important element of Sheffield life. Not only were football and cricket teams formed, but they were accompanied by swimming teams, by crown green bowling competitions and road running and walking

LEFT: **THE OLD STAND AND PAVILION, BRAMALL LANE.** Bramall Lane was originally a cricket ground. Yorkshire County Cricket Club was founded in Sheffield in 1863 and county matches were played at Bramall Lane for more than a century. It became Sheffield United's football ground in 1889.

BELOW: **BARNES GREEN CRICKET TEAM, 1910.** The team, from a hamlet between High Green and Grenoside, pose in a typically crisp photograph by Arnie Greaves, an outstanding local photographer.

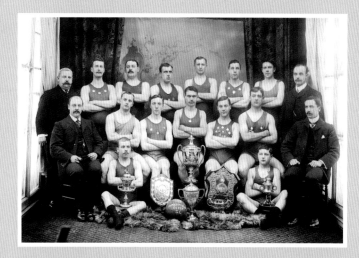

ABOVE: **THE OTTER SWIMMING TEAM, EARLY 1900S.** Swimming teams were formed after the opening of public swimming baths. The first Corporation swimming baths were opened in 1869 and in 1895 they took over Glossop Road swimming and Turkish baths that had been opened in 1836.

BELOW: **SHEFFIELD UNITED FOOTBALL TEAM, 1899.** The bowler- and top-hatted Sheffield United players show off the FA Cup that they had won decisively at Crystal Palace against Derby County before a crowd of 74,000, including the Prime Minister, AJ Balfour. Although behind 1-0 at half-time, a scintillating second-half display saw them score four times to inflict on Derby their second successive Cup Final defeat.

Back Row (left to right): Messrs. A. G. W. Dronfield, J. Holmes, A. J. Dickinson, J. C. Clegg, H. Nixon, J. Thackray, ——. Ellis, T. Lee, W. Turner, W. F. Wardley. *Middle Row:* J. Davis (asst. trainer), H. Newbould, H. Davis, Brittleton, Layton, Lyall, Bartlett, Slavin, Burton, Foxall, P. Frith (trainer). *Front Row:* Bradshaw, Chapman, A. Wilson, T. Crawshaw, Stewart, G. Simpson, and Maxwell.

ABOVE: **TWO LOCAL FOOTBALL TEAMS.** Many different organisations produced their sports teams: there were village teams, works teams, church and chapel teams and public house teams. TOP: **TINSLEY CHURCH SCHOOL FOOTBALL TEAM** about 1910; and BOTTOM: **ECCLESFIELD UNITED FOOTBALL TEAM**, 1920s.

LEFT: **SHEFFIELD WEDNESDAY FOOTBALL TEAM, 1907.** The playing squad and officials proudly pose with the FA Cup that they had won that year. In a tight game they had beaten Everton 2-1 at Crystal Palace before a crowd of 84,000.

SHEFFIELD AT WAR

Sheffield lies far from the coast and during the Second World War contained no important military bases. But the city was an important cog in the country's war effort, producing in its works munitions and every conceivable item of war equipment

LEFT: **THE HOME GUARD.** The first volunteer in Sheffield had signed up at a police station within four minutes of the announcement of the formation of the Home Guard on the radio in May 1940.

BELOW: **HIGH STREET** during the first part of Sheffield's blitz, on the night and early morning of Thursday and Friday December 12-13, 1940. Another heavy raid took place on the night of Sunday December 15. There were 589 deaths.

ABOVE: **EVACUEES, 1939.** Labelled evacuees leave from Victoria Station. Evacuation to the countryside and small towns was the practical solution to protecting children from bombing. For some it was a wonderful experience, for others pure misery.

BELOW: **TRYING ON GAS MASKS.** They were carried everywhere slung over the shoulder in a cardboard box or a canvas bag. And schoolchildren had to practice putting them on quickly. Posters warned that "Hitler would send no warning – always carry your gas mask".

RIGHT: Looking at the scene of bomb devastation across **ANGEL STREET** after some clearing up had taken place. The tall white building in the right background is Burton's the tailors.

BELOW: **THE MARPLES HOTEL, 13 DECEMBER 1940.** It has been estimated that between 50 and 70 people were killed from a direct hit at 11.44pm on Thursday December 12. The photograph shows the tangled remains of the Marples Hotel in the foreground and in the background are the ruins of C&A Modes.

ABOVE: **VE CELEBRATIONS.** An informal celebration of VE Day in May 1945 in Rushdale Avenue, Meersbrook, with the Union Jack well in evidence. These children would probably all have eventually sat down to a formal street tea-party followed by sports and games.

PEOPLE AND PLACES

This section takes the reader on an extensive tour of the city in the period from the 1880s to the 1950s, looking at the unusual, the everyday and the memorable

LEFT AND ABOVE: Old houses great and small dot the landscape in and around Sheffield. Above is **BEAUCHIEF HALL**, built in the 17th century as the mansion of the Pegge family on land they acquired after the dissolution of Beauchief Abbey. Left is the **WATCH HOUSE** at Bradfield. This house, set at the entrance to the churchyard, was built in about 1830 as a lookout point to discourage bodysnatchers!

ABOVE: **THE LEPPING STONES AT WADSLEY** over the River Don. "Lepping" is a corruption of "Leaping". These stepping stones, now gone, were used by generations making their way into Sheffield from Wadsley, Birley Carr and Grenoside.

ABOVE: **HILLSBOROUGH BOARD SCHOOL,** *c* 1900. Sturdy stone-built National and Board schools sprang up in all parts of the city during its rapid expansion in the 19th century.

ABOVE LEFT: **W H STEVENSON'S GREENGROCERY, 1930S.** There were no superstores until the 1960s and before that you bought your fruit and vegetables at your neighbourhood greengrocer's store, with its enticing and beautifully arranged window display, like this one on Dykes Lane, Hillsborough.

ABOVE: **GREAVES' CYCLE SHOP, EARLY 1900S.** The "cycling craze" was still at its height when the photograph was taken and no doubt this shop in Middlewood Road, Hillsborough did a roaring trade.

ABOVE: **THE CINEMA HOUSE, ECCLESFIELD.** This cinema, built in 1920 and demolished in the early 1970s, had on each side of the main entrance two shops, one of which sold sweets and chocolates and stayed open until late in the evening to serve the cinemagoers.

RIGHT: **ST MARY'S LANE, ECCLESFIELD, _c_ 1900.** The view shows the western end of the village looking towards the Perpendicular-style church, rebuilt about the year 1500. The parish of Ecclesfield originally covered 78 square miles and the church became known as the "Mynster of the Moors".

ABOVE: BURNCROSS WEDDING, 1910. Another Arnie Greaves photograph, this time of the wedding of Sam Ashforth and Elsie Matthews. Elsie's parents, seated on either side of the bride and groom, kept the Crown and Cushion Inn.

E.L.S. 234-18. Station Road, Chapeltown.

ABOVE: STATION ROAD, CHAPELTOWN, 1915. In the foreground is the Moorish style Picture House that was opened on 23 December 1912. It had the same chief projectionist, Alfred Dawson, from the day it opened in 1912 until 1954. It closed in 1963.

Old Toll Bar, Pitsmoor. M 25.248.

ABOVE: THE TOLL HOUSE, PITSMOOR, *c* 1900. This toll house, which still survives, was built in 1827 on the Sheffield, Barnsley & Wakefield turnpike road at the junction of Pitsmoor Road and Burngreave Road. It controlled two gates until it was closed in 1876.

RIGHT: COWLEY MANOR, CHAPELTOWN, 1900. This is a late 16th- or early 17th-century house built by the Earl of Shrewsbury. It replaced a medieval manor house described by a 17th century surveyor as "a stately castle-like house moated about".

RIGHT: **HIGH GREEN INFANTS SCHOOL, 1893.** The infants group, beautifully turned out with the girls in their white smocks and wearing bonnets, keep quite still under the watchful eye of the headteacher, Miss Annie Williams, standing on the left.

LEFT: **LOW NEWBIGGIN, EARLY 1920S.** With an old colliery spoil heap in the background Jack Jeffries takes his younger brothers for a ride in a splendid goat cart.

BELOW: **ABBEYFIELD PARK,** *c* **1910.** Abbeyfield Park, a small park in Burngreave Road, was formerly the grounds of Abbeyfield House, which in the second half of the 19th century was the home of the Wake family, Sheffield solicitors. It became a public park in 1909. The boating lake has now been filled in.

ABOVE LEFT: **WHIT WALK, DARNALL, EARLY 1900S.** Children from Holy Trinity Church, dressed in their Whitsuntide Sunday best, pose in front of their church banner. Members of the local scout group stand to attention in their smart uniforms.

ABOVE: **BURNGREAVE ROAD, *c* 1910.** There can be no doubt when the photograph was taken. The style of clothing, the gas lamp, the horse trough and evidence that the road was on one of the relatively new electric tram routes all suggest the end of the Edwardian period.

ABOVE: **WOODBURN ROAD, WESLEYAN REFORM CHAPEL, ATTERCLIFFE, 1912.** Loaves are being distributed to the wives of striking miners. The strike was a successful minimum wage strike that involved all the coalfields. The miners in this case probably worked at the nearby Nunnery Colliery.

RIGHT: **ATTERCLIFFE ROAD, EARLY 1900S.** A tram passes a butcher's cart and a refuse cart on this busy main road. By 1909 it was possible to travel by tram from the western suburbs of Sheffield via Attercliffe, as far as Denaby Main, nearly six miles beyond Rotherham.

ABOVE: **DARNALL CINEMA.** Opened in 1913, this cinema on Catcliffe Road was built by George Payling, a local builder. It closed in 1957. In its early years a good night out could be had at the "popular prices of 2d, 4d and 6d".

ABOVE: **COLLEGIATE HALL, ECCLESALL ROAD, EARLY 1900S.** Originally part of the Collegiate School founded in 1836, it merged with the Royal Grammar School in 1884. It eventually became a teachers' training college and is now part of Sheffield Hallam University.

ABOVE: **E M TAYLOR'S BUTCHER'S SHOP, EARLY 1900S.** Located on Coleridge Road, Attercliffe Common, this busy road at this time also had several grocers, a greengrocer, tailor, dressmaker, milk seller, coal dealer and a post office.

ABOVE: **ECCLESALL ROAD, c 1910.** The view shows the road near its junction with Brocco Bank and Rustlings Road at Hunter's Bar. This very busy tram route not only led to residential suburbs but also to Endcliffe Park and Whiteley Woods, two of the most popular open spaces in the city.

LEFT: **HUNTER'S BAR TOLL HOUSE, 1884.** The toll house was opened in 1811 on the new Ecclesall Road heading towards the Peak District. It closed on October 31 1884 and the horse bus on the left was the last vehicle to pay a toll.

ABOVE LEFT: HUNTER'S BAR, 1930S.
This view looks back along Ecclesall Road towards the city centre. In the extreme right foreground is one of the 120 famous Sheffield police boxes introduced by Chief Constable Percy Sillitoe in October 1928.

ABOVE: ECCLESALL WOODS, *c* 1910.
Ecclesall Woods are the largest area (*c* 300 acres) of ancient woodland in Sheffield. The city has nearly 80 ancient woodlands (known to have already been in existence in 1600). It is the best-wooded city in the country.

ABOVE: POMONA HOTEL, *c* 1910.
A crowd poses for the photographer outside the Pomona Hotel on Ecclesall Road. The cyclists, from Sharrow C(ycling) C(lub), have probably met here prior to a day out in the Peak District.

RIGHT: RANMOOR ROAD, RANMOOR, *c* 1910. The view is of the main road through what John Betjeman described as one of his favourite Victorian suburbs. Burgon & Co were a well-known Sheffield firm of grocers, tea, coffee and spice merchants with several shops dotted around the city.

LEFT: **BULL'S HEAD HOTEL, FULWOOD ROAD**, *c* 1900. This substantial hotel reflects the middle-class suburb in which it was situated. Of equal interest is the perambulator being wheeled down the road, probably by a nanny working for one of the more affluent families of the area.

BELOW: **CASTLE INN, TWENTYWELL LANE, BEAUCHIEF**, *c* 1910. "Sparkling Ales and Beers" were on offer at the Castle Inn, but nevertheless many of its male customers were not prepared to wait. Instead they were going to set off on an outing.

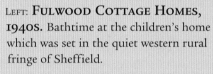

LEFT: **FULWOOD COTTAGE HOMES, 1940S.** Bathtime at the children's home which was set in the quiet western rural fringe of Sheffield.

BELOW: **HIGH-RISE TOWER BLOCKS, NETHERTHORPE, 1950S.** Post-war housing development went on at a rapid pace to replace slums and houses destroyed or badly damaged during the Blitz. By 1969, of the 186,000 houses in the city, 69,000 were Council-owned.

THE SURROUNDING COUNTRYSIDE

The physical setting of Sheffield is equalled by no other British city. It is enveloped in the west by very extensive tracts of moorland and upland pasture, cut by deep attractive valleys, all within the boundaries of the modern city

ABOVE: **DAMFLASK RESERVOIR.** The construction of a dozen reservoirs in the steep-sided valleys to the west of the city in the late 19th and early 20th centuries created Sheffield's own "lake district" with facilities for various kinds of water-based recreation.

ABOVE: **STANAGE EDGE.** Lying on the western edge of Hallam Moors at 1400ft (426m) with magnificent views over the Derwent valley, Stanage Edge was a magnet for walkers, including members of the widely-supported Sheffield Clarion Ramblers, founded in 1900.

RIGHT: **WYMING BROOK, 1905.** Located in the upper Rivelin valley, Wyming Brook has long held a spell over Sheffielders thinking of heading for the countryside on bright summer days and it appeared on many Edwardian postcards.

First published in 2005 by Myriad Books Limited
35 Bishopsthorpe Road, London SE26 4PA

All photographs copyright © Sheffield Archives and Local Studies Library except those on the title page and pages 2 (bottom); 5 (bottom right); 6 (all); 7 (centre left); 8 (top right); 12 (centre left and centre right); 14 (top right; centre right; bottom left) 15 (top right and bottom); 16 (top left); 24 (top left); 25 (centre left) 29 (bottom); 30 (top right); 31 (bottom) and 32 (bottom) which are from Joan and Melvyn Jones' personal collection and those on pages 9 (top right), 15 (centre); 18 (top and bottom right); 19 (top left and bottom left); 20 (bottom right); 21 (centre right); 25 (bottom); 26 (top left and top right and bottom right); 27 (top left and top right) which are copyright Chapeltown and High Green Archive.

Text copyright © Melvyn Jones

Melvyn Jones has asserted his right under the Copyright, Designs and Patents Act 1998 to be identified as the author of this work.

ISBN 1 904 736 73 4

Designed by Jerry Goldie Graphic Design

Printed in China

www.myriadbooks.com